A LOOK AT YOUR GOVERNMENT

WHY DO WE VOTE?

BY SANTANA HUNT

Gareth Stevens PUBLISHING

CRASHCOURSE

Please visit our website, www.garethstevens.com. For a free color catalog of all our high-quality books, call toll free 1-800-542-2595 or fax 1-877-542-2596.

Cataloging-in-Publication Data
Names: Hunt, Santana.
Title: Why do we vote? / Santana Hunt.
Description: New York : Gareth Stevens Publishing, 2018. | Series: A look at your government | Includes index.
Identifiers: ISBN 9781482460674 (pbk.) | ISBN 9781482460698 (library bound) | ISBN 9781482460681 (6 pack)
Subjects: LCSH: Elections--United States--Juvenile literature. | Voting--United States--Juvenile literature.
Classification: LCC JK1978.H83 2018 | DDC 324.60973--dc23

First Edition

Published in 2018 by
Gareth Stevens Publishing
111 East 14th Street, Suite 349
New York, NY 10003

Editor: Kristen Nelson
Designer: Samantha DeMartin

Photo credits: Cover, p. 1 Blend Images - Hill Street Studios/Getty Images; series art MaxyM/Shutterstock.com; p. 5 Stock Montage/Archive Photos/Getty Images; p. 7 Orhan Cam/Shutterstock.com; p. 9 Family Business/Shutterstock.com; p. 11 a katz/Shutterstock.com; p. 13 Brent Lewis/Denver Post/Getty Images; p. 15 Douglas Graham/CQ-Roll Call Group/Getty Images; p. 17 (voters) Burlingham/Shutterstock.com; p. 17 (map) Electric_Crayon/Getty Images; p. 19 Lisa F. Young/Shutterstock.com; p. 21 Hero Images/Hero Images/Getty Images; pp. 23, 30 (1870) courtesy of the Library of Congress; p. 25 Barry Williams/Getty Images News/Getty Images; pp. 27, 29 (bottom) Joseph Sohm/Shutterstock.com; p. 29 (top) Ken Wolter/Shutterstock.com; p. 30 (I Voted sticker) icemanj/Shutterstock.com; p. 30 (1920) Everett Historical/Shutterstock.com; p. 30 (1965) Davepape/Wikimedia Commons; p. 30 (1971) Bettmann/Bettmann/Getty Images.

Printed in the United States of America

CPSIA compliance information: Batch #CS17GS: For further information contact Gareth Stevens, New York, New York at 1-800-542-2595.

CONTENTS

Words in the glossary appear in **bold** type the first time they are used in the text.

A Right from the Start

One reason the American **colonists** wanted freedom from Great Britain was because they didn't get a say in their government. That's why the Founding Fathers wanted to allow those living in the new United States to have a vote!

MAKE THE GRADE

At first, most states only gave white men over age 21 the right to vote. Today, **citizens** over age 18 can vote.

And to the Republic...

The United States is a republic. In this type of government, citizens vote for people to **represent** them. In the United States, these representatives serve in Congress. Congress is made up of the House of Representatives and the Senate.

MAKE THE GRADE

In a republic, the people also vote for a leader, such as the president.

Elections in the United States

The act of voting is called an election. There are two main kinds of elections in the United States. In a primary, a **candidate** is chosen from many candidates trying to represent a political party in the general election.

MAKE THE GRADE

Political parties are groups of people who share beliefs about how the government should be run. The Democrats and Republicans are the two main political parties in the United States.

In a general election, voters choose from the winners of the political parties' primaries. The winner of a general election then takes on the position he or she was running for, such as mayor.

MAKE THE GRADE

Members of political parties only vote for candidates within their party during a primary election. Anyone can vote for any candidate in the general election.

MAYOR
BILL DE BLASIO

At All Levels

Voters choose those who will represent them in the local, state, and **federal** government. No matter what part of government you're voting for, it's important to know what candidates stand for. The choices an elected **official** makes can affect your life.

MAKE THE GRADE

Propositions, or measures that could change state laws, are often voted on during local and state elections, too.

Local and state elections decide who will run the schools, have a say in town laws, and give money to businesses. Congressional elections decide who will take the needs of the state to the federal government.

MAKE THE GRADE

Every elected official serves a certain number of years in office, called a term. In many cases, they can serve more than one term.

REPRESENTATIVE
CATHY MCMORRIS RODGERS

Votes for President

With one exception, elections in the United States are decided by the popular vote, or the sum of the individual votes of a place. The Electoral College **process**, however, elects the US president and vice president.

MAKE THE GRADE

The Electoral College is made up of people called electors who promise to vote for a certain candidate. When citizens vote for president, they're actually voting for these electors.

US Electoral Votes by State

Voter Turnout

Millions of Americans can vote, but many don't! In fact, many elections see less than half of **eligible** voters voting. Voter turnout, or how many people show up to vote, can greatly affect the outcome of an election.

MAKE THE GRADE

In the United States, young people tend to vote less than older people.

One reason people might not vote is because they aren't registered, or signed up, to do so. In some states, there are laws that say people must register months before an election! Some think these laws keep voter turnout low.

MAKE THE GRADE

When voters register to vote, they can join a political party. They don't have to, but if they do, they can vote in that party's primary elections.

I VOTED
I VOTED

Voting Rights

At times in US history, certain groups of people have been kept from voting because of **discrimination**. Some places made African American voters take a test or pay to vote. People have tried to keep other **minority groups** from voting, too.

MAKE THE GRADE

Today, there are commonly still more white voters than other groups. Many people are hard at work to register more minority voters.

In 1965, the Voting Rights Act tried to stop voting discrimination. It made it illegal to stop someone from voting because of race. It also made testing any voters before they voted illegal. Today, some voting discrimination still happens.

MAKE THE GRADE

Much of the voter discrimination was in the South. The Voting Rights Act of 1965 made voter turnout in the South rise by a lot.

Tatnall St SW
CYNTHIA
McKinney
CONGRESS
I VOTED! 2 B CONT...
LEST WE FORGET
KEEP THE VOTE ALIVE!
RAINBOW PUSH COALITION

VOTE FOR CHANGE

An important reason we vote is to cause change. Citizens' votes may not only choose leaders, but also choose to change the leaders representing them. If voters aren't happy with what the government is doing, they can use their votes to speak up!

MAKE THE GRADE

Many people believe it's their duty as US citizens to know about candidates and vote. It makes them feel part of the political process!

Supporting a candidate doesn't do much if you don't cast a vote on election day! It's uncommon for a single vote to decide an election. But many people voting together can make a difference.

MAKE THE GRADE

A long time ago, political parties used to give voters money, food, or even a live pig to vote for the candidate they wanted!

I
Voted
VOTE
HERE

HISTORY OF US VOTING RIGHTS

1870

African American men are given the right to vote.

1920

Women are given the right to vote.

1965

The Voting Rights Act states no one can be denied the right to vote based on race, faith, sex, or abilities.

1971

The voting age is lowered to 18.

GLOSSARY

candidate: someone who runs for a public office

citizen: someone who lives in a country legally and has certain rights

colonist: someone who lives in a colony, or a piece of land under the control of another country

discrimination: unfairly treating people unequally because of their race or beliefs

eligible: fit to be chosen

federal: having to do with the national government

minority group: a small group of people who are not part of the main group of a society. In the United States, African Americans, Native Americans, Latinos, and the poor are minority groups.

official: someone who holds a leadership position

process: a series of steps or actions taken to complete something

represent: to stand for. A person who represents is a representative.

FOR MORE INFORMATION

Books

Lansford, Tom. *Political Participation and Voting Rights.* Broomall, PA: Mason Crest, 2017.

Weiss, Nancy E. *Asking Questions About Political Campaigns.* Ann Arbor, MI: Cherry Lake Publishing, 2016.

Websites

PBS Kids: The Democracy Project

pbskids.org/democracy/vote/

Learn about how the election process works.

Publisher's note to educators and parents: Our editors have carefully reviewed these websites to ensure that they are suitable for students. Many websites change frequently, however, and we cannot guarantee that a site's future contents will continue to meet our high standards of quality and educational value. Be advised that students should be closely supervised whenever they access the Internet.

INDEX